# CINCINNATI
# REDS

by Marty Gitlin

Published by ABDO Publishing Company, 8000 West 78th Street, Edina, Minnesota 55439. Copyright © 2011 by Abdo Consulting Group, Inc. International copyrights reserved in all countries. No part of this book may be reproduced in any form without written permission from the publisher. SportsZone™ is a trademark and logo of ABDO Publishing Company.

Printed in the United States of America,
North Mankato, Minnesota
112010
012011

Editor: Chrös McDougall
Copy Editor: Nicholas Cafarelli
Interior Design and Production: Carol Castro
Cover Design: Kazuko Collins

**Photo Credits:** Al Behrman/AP Images, cover, 47; AP Images, 1, 7, 9, 18, 21, 23, 25, 26, 28, 30, 33, 37, 42 (middle and bottom), 43 (top); Ron Frehm/AP Images, 4, 43 (middle); Rusty Kennedy/AP Images, 11; Library of Congress, 12, 15, 17, 42 (top); Tom Uhlman/AP Images, 34; Paul Sakuma/AP Images, 38; Matt Slocum/AP Images, 41, 43 (bottom); Gene J. Puskar/AP Images, 44

**Library of Congress Cataloging-in-Publication Data**
Gitlin, Marty.
  Cincinnati Reds / by Marty Gitlin.
      p. cm. — (Inside MLB)
  ISBN 978-1-61714-040-2
  1. Cincinnati Reds (Baseball team)—History—Juvenile literature. I. Title.
  GV875.C65G58 2011
  796.357'640977178—dc22
                              2010036558

# TABLE OF CONTENTS

# CHAPTER 1

# THE BIG RED MACHINE

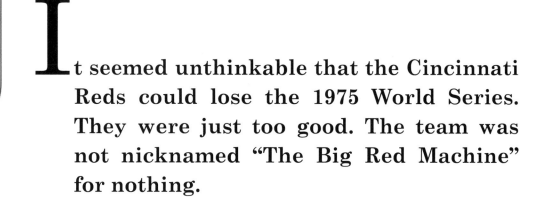

I t seemed unthinkable that the Cincinnati Reds could lose the 1975 World Series. They were just too good. The team was not nicknamed "The Big Red Machine" for nothing.

The 1975 Reds had one of the strongest lineups in baseball history. Third baseman Pete Rose would later become Major League Baseball's (MLB) career hits leader. In 1975, he combined with first baseman Tony Perez, outfielder George Foster, catcher Johnny Bench, and second baseman Joe Morgan to strike fear into opposing pitchers. They led the Reds to 108 wins that season. That was the highest total in the National League (NL) in 66 years.

Yet in the sixth inning of the seventh game of the World Series, the Reds appeared doomed—again.

Pete Rose was one of the top batters in baseball history. He led the NL in hits seven times and finished his career as baseball's all-time hit leader.

The Reds had a reputation of being a powerhouse during the regular season. They had made the playoffs in three of the past five years. But they fell short of winning the World Series each time. Now it appeared they were about to disappoint again. They trailed the Boston Red Sox 3–0 in the top of the sixth inning.

But then the Reds started to look like the team that had dominated the regular season. Their bullpen had shut down the Red Sox's bats in the fifth. Then Perez blasted a two-run home run in the sixth. Rose added a single that drove in the tying run in the seventh.

The score remained tied until the ninth inning. Morgan stepped to the plate with runners on first and second and two outs. He proceeded to hit a bloop single up the middle, driving in the go-ahead run. Reds reliever Will McEnaney then blanked the Sox in the bottom of the inning. Finally, the Reds had won their first World Series title since 1940.

The parade festivities the following day featured beloved manager Sparky Anderson. A *Sports Illustrated* reporter described the jubilation from early that morning.

"It was a bright, joyous day in Cincinnati, and the streets

## Joe Morgan

Reds second baseman Joe Morgan looked odd at the plate. He flapped his left arm like a chicken as he awaited the pitch to make certain he kept his elbow up. But nobody questioned the results. Morgan blossomed into a Hall of Famer upon his arrival in Cincinnati in 1972. He scored at least 107 runs and stole an average of 60 bases in the next six seasons. He won the NL Most Valuable Player (MVP) Award in both 1975 and 1976. Morgan later spent 21 seasons calling ESPN's Sunday Night Baseball.

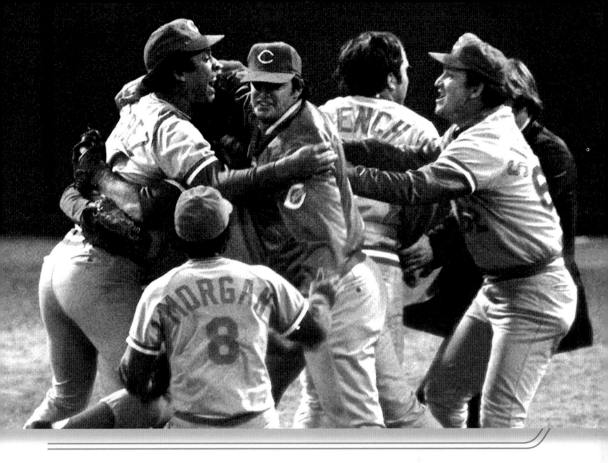

The Cincinnati Reds celebrate after beating the Boston Red Sox to win the 1975 World Series.

were already alive with celebrants," he wrote. "Flakes of ticker tape, calendar pads, stationery, toilet paper floated lazily from upper-story windows of downtown buildings. . . . By noon, townspeople had overflowed Fountain Square.

"Youngsters scaled trees, statues, fences, lampposts to see the parade. . . . As the Reds arrived via another route, secretaries in office buildings jumped from their desks and waved from behind windows."

The writer continued, "Anderson held his arms aloft and, on his arrival at the podium, bent to embrace a startled little boy, a gesture that

## SUPER SPARKY

Sparky Anderson had no managerial experience when Reds general manager Bob Howsam interviewed him after the 1969 season. Yet Howsam had a feeling that Anderson could thrive as the team's manager. So he took a chance and hired him to take over the young, talented team. "I needed a leader, somebody to get all that ability out of our players," Howsam said.

He made a good choice. Anderson guided the Reds to a franchise-best 102–60 record and the NL pennant in 1970. He led them to the World Series again in 1972 before earning titles in 1975 and 1976. His Reds teams won at least 88 games in eight of the nine years he served as manager.

Anderson left the Reds after refusing to accept changes in his coaching staff following the 1978 season. He was sorely missed as he managed the Detroit Tigers to the 1984 World Series title.

earned him even more affection from the crowd."

That affection for Anderson and his team grew the following season. The Big Red Machine led the league in runs, hits, doubles, triples, home runs, stolen bases, and batting average in 1976. Five starters hit .300 or better as the Reds averaged 5.3 runs per game.

Many believe that Bench was the best hitting catcher in baseball history. But he was not one of those .300 hitters in 1976. In fact, he suffered through his worst year offensively that season. But he was ready when the Reds faced the New York Yankees in the World Series. He batted .533 for the Series and slugged two home runs in Game 4 as the Reds completed an unlikely sweep to win their second World Series in a row.

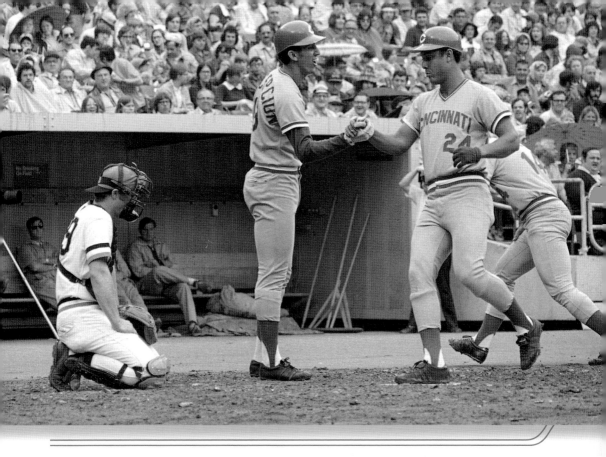

Dave Concepcion, *left*, greets Tony Perez after Perez hit a grand slam during the 1973 season.

"It was neat to know we whipped up on New York," Bench recalled years later. "It happened so quick, it seemed like it was over before you knew it. It was special."

The Reds pitchers starred, too. They even managed to steal some of the spotlight in the 1976 Series. The Reds

## Riverfront Stadium

*The Reds moved to Riverfront Stadium in June 1970. Fans packed the stadium during the championship years of 1975 and 1976. The attendance mark was shattered in 1975 with a total of 2,315,603 fans pouring through the gates. It was broken again in 1976 with a mark of 2,629,708.*

yielded just eight runs in the four games against the high-powered Yankees.

The team remained strong through 1981. The Reds won at least 88 games every year from 1977 to 1980 and earned a division crown in 1979. Foster was particularly dominant. He hit a league-high 52 home runs and had 149 runs batted in (RBIs) in 1977. He also won the NL MVP Award that year.

But greatness rarely lasts in baseball. Players such as Bench, Morgan, Rose, and Foster eventually left. In 1982, the Reds finished with the worst record in the NL. It was a sudden and disturbing drop for the oldest professional team in America. The Big Red Machine soon became another one of many treasured memories for the storied franchise.

## The Ace

The Big Red Machine was known for its hitting, but several strong seasons from starting pitchers helped the team win pennants. And the best was Don Gullett. The left-hander led the NL in winning percentage in 1971 and compiled a record of 61–26 from 1973 through 1976. He led the Reds with a 2.42 earned-run average (ERA) in 1975.

George Foster batted .320 and hit 52 home runs on his way to winning the 1977 NL MVP Award.

# CHAPTER 2

# THE FIRST PROS

**T**he Civil War had only ended four years before the first professional team graced a baseball diamond. That team was the Cincinnati Red Stockings. They beat the Mutuals of New York, 17–8, on November 6, 1869. That completed their first season with a perfect 57–0 record.

The Red Stockings won their first 24 games the next year. Then, in 1876, Cincinnati became a charter member of the National League. The team was kicked out of the NL four years later, however. It refused to stop playing home games on Sundays and to stop selling beer at the ballpark.

The Reds of today can officially be traced back to 1882, when a new team called the Red Stockings began playing in the upstart American Association. They enjoyed a successful run in the league. The Red Stockings won the title in 1882 and finished with a winning record in six of the next seven seasons.

Hod Eller went 19–9 with a 2.39 ERA during the Reds' 1919 World Series championship season.

Cincinnati was welcomed back into the NL in 1890 and went on to finish 77–55. But the inconsistency that would haunt them through most of their existence soon began to appear. The team, now called the Reds, had records of .500 or better every year but three from 1892 to 1905. Then they had just one winning season from 1906 through 1916. They

did not finish higher than third place from 1886 through 1918.

The Reds did not have many star players in that era. But the team did manage to put together an occasional great season. Among the great players was outfielder Cy Seymour. He led the NL in batting average (.377), hits (219), doubles (40), triples (21), and RBIs (121) in 1905.

The team had a breakthrough in 1919. Under first-year manager Pat Moran, the Reds won the pennant with a 96–44 record. Outfielder Edd Roush led the offense. He had a .321 average and drove in 71 runs. But it was the finest pitching staff in the NL that carried the Reds to the championship. Pitchers Hod Eller, Dutch Ruether, and Slim Sallee combined to go 59–22. No starting pitcher had an ERA above 2.39.

## Edd Roush

The Reds of the early twentieth century featured few premier players. The rosters of even their best teams were not dotted with stars. Outfielder Edd Roush was the exception. Roush played 11 seasons in Cincinnati beginning in 1916. He was easily the team's best all-around player. He led the NL in batting average in 1917 and 1919, in doubles in 1923, and in triples in 1924. He hit over .300 every year he played with the Reds. He finished his career with the Reds in 1931. He eventually landed in the Baseball Hall of Fame.

Hall of Famer Christy Mathewson, contributing to the Red Cross War Fund, won in his only start for the Reds in 1916. He became manager in 1917.

The Reds had a strong regular season. But they were considered underdogs to the American League (AL) champion Chicago White Sox in the best-of-nine 1919 World Series. However, the Reds quickly showed they were the better team. Ruether, Sallee, Eller, and Jimmy Ring gave up a

## Name Change

*The word "red" has always been part of the nickname of Cincinnati's baseball team. But there have been a few variations. The team was known as the Red Stockings during their time in the American Association through 1889. And from 1954 to 1959, their name was officially changed to the "Redlegs." Why? Because the team didn't want to be associated with Communists, who were referred to in slang as "Reds."*

combined three runs as the Reds took a 4–1 lead in games. The White Sox won the next two games. But Eller clinched the title with a 10–5 victory in Game 8.

The dominant pitching that guided the Reds through the regular season showed up in force at the World Series. Ring allowed just one run in 14 innings. The entire staff recorded an ERA of 1.63 in the eight-game series.

## Opening Day

Cincinnati is famous for its enthusiastic Opening Day. In fact, the Reds remain the only team in MLB to always play their first game of the year at home. The city holds a grand parade every year to kick off the baseball season. That tradition began in 1891, when owner John T. Brush organized the event. It included a military band and two large horse-drawn wagons that pulled players from the Reds and the Cleveland Spiders, their opponent that day.

However, the Reds—and baseball—were soon dealt some shocking news. While the Reds were playing to win the 1919 World Series, the White Sox were playing to lose it. People began to suspect that some key White Sox players had accepted bribes to lose the Series on purpose. Those players admitted they had done so after the 1920 season. In what became forever known as the Black Sox Scandal, the Reds did not win the World Series solely through their own efforts.

Still, many believed that the Reds would have won the title anyway. After all, the Reds won eight more games than the White Sox during the regular season. Roush later claimed that the White Sox threw only the first game of the World Series. Author and Cincinnati native William A. Cook believed that the Reds would

August Herrmann, *right*, shown meeting with a concessionaire, was president of the Reds from 1902 to 1927.

have emerged with the championship in an honest series.

"I've never denied there was a scandal," Cook said, "but I'm convinced some of the Series was played [honestly]. It didn't make any difference. I've gone game by game, pitch by pitch, and I've found that the Reds would have won anyway."

Nobody knows for sure. But what is certain is that the Reds and their fans would have to wait another 21 years to celebrate a World Series title that nobody questioned.

CHAPTER **3**

# ONE GOOD DECADE, ONE BAD

**T**he Reds sought an untainted World Series title after the Black Sox Scandal was exposed. They remained a strong team after that 1919 season. But they never could win enough games to claim another NL pennant.

The Reds were generally a winning team during the early 1920s, but they always fell short of the pennant. The 1926 season was particularly frustrating for the team. The Reds were in first place until they lost six games in a row in late September.

But the Reds of the 1920s featured a number of strong hitters. They included Edd Roush, first baseman Jake Daubert, second baseman Hughie Critz, outfielders George Burns, George Harper, and Pat Duncan, catcher Bubbles Hargrave, and third baseman Babe Pinelli.

Hall of Fame left-hander Eppa Rixey played for the Reds from 1921 to 1933. He led the NL with 25 wins in 1922.

The starting pitching remained strong behind Eppa Rixey, Pete Donohue, Carl Mays, and Dolf Luque.

The US economy collapsed in 1929 and the country fell into the Great Depression. The Reds collapsed that year, as well. They had a 78–74 record in 1928. That was followed by nine losing seasons. From 1929 to 1937, the Reds finished 30 or more games out of first place eight times. It was a miserable time for baseball in Cincinnati.

The fans could hardly afford to attend baseball games during these times. They had little interest in spending whatever money they had to watch bad Reds teams. Season attendance dropped to just more than 200,000 by the early 1930s.

Another poor year in 1938 seemed inevitable. But the Reds surprisingly became contenders. Catcher Ernie Lombardi batted .342. He combined with first baseman Frank McCormick and outfielder Ival Goodman for 293 RBIs. Meanwhile, pitchers Paul Derringer and Johnny Vander Meer blossomed. They won 36 games between them. The 1938 Reds placed fourth in the NL.

A year later they placed first. Several players contributed to the pennant run in 1939. However, three stood out more than the rest. McCormick led the offense with a .332 average

During the 1938 season, Johnny Vander Meer threw the only back-to-back no-hitters in major league history.

and 128 RBIs. Pitcher Bucky Walters emerged to compile a 27–11 record and a 2.29 ERA. Derringer added 25 victories to complete a premier one-two pitching punch. But the Reds were not ready to topple the mighty New York Yankees in the World Series. They scored just eight runs in four straight losses.

McCormick played well again in 1940. He batted .309 and racked up 127 RBIs to win the NL MVP Award. He also received help from Lombardi as

## DOUBLE NO-NO

Reds left-hander Johnny Vander Meer became the only major league pitcher to throw successive no-hitters when he did so in 1938. The first was a 3–0 win over the Boston Bees at Crosley Field on June 11. The second was recorded on June 15 in the first night game at Brooklyn's Ebbets Field. Vander Meer walked eight batters, but managed to complete a 6–0 victory over the Dodgers. He walked the bases loaded in the ninth inning before escaping with the no-hitter.

After the game, the Reds asked Vander Meer to change his uniform number to 00 to honor his back-to-back no-hitters, but he declined. He told the Associated Press after the season that "all the publicity, the attention, the interviews, the photographs, were too much for me." Vander Meer allowed only one run on four hits in his next game. He also tossed three scoreless innings in the NL's victory in the All-Star Game.

well as second baseman Lonny Frey and third baseman Billy Werber. They combined to score 207 runs. Walters and Derringer again pitched like aces as the Reds rolled to their second consecutive NL pennant.

The Reds battled the Detroit Tigers in the 1940 World Series. The Tigers won the first, third, and fifth games. But the Reds bounced back each time. They won the second, fourth, and sixth games. Walters pitched a five-hit shutout for a 4–0 victory in Game 6.

That set up a Game 7 showdown for the title. The Reds trailed Tigers ace Bobo Newsom, 1–0, in the seventh inning of Game 7. But doubles by McCormick and Jimmy Ripple and a sacrifice fly by Billy Myers gave the Reds a 2–1 lead. Derringer shut out

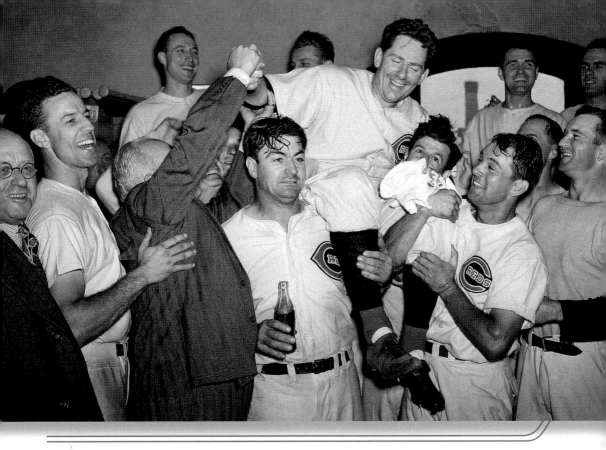

Reds players hoist winning pitcher Paul Derringer on their shoulders after they beat the Detroit Tigers to win the 1940 World Series title.

the Tigers the rest of the way to give his team its first untarnished world title. The fans in Cincinnati went wild.

"The civic madness started at Crosley Field a split second after the final out and, spreading like chicken pox in a playground, swept the entire city, from suburb to suburb

## Just a Kid

*With several Reds players overseas fighting in World War II in 1944, the Reds used the youngest player to ever don a major league uniform. On June 10 of that year, 15-year-old Joe Nuxhall pitched in an 18–0 loss to the St. Louis Cardinals. Nuxhall retired just two batters while giving up five runs in his debut. He did not pitch for the Reds again until eight years later.*

and city limit to city limit," explained one story in the *Cincinnati Enquirer*. "Automobile horns, thousands of them, played their sweet symphonies; factory whistles screamed . . . thousands of persons just walked around yelling, singing, whistling and clapping hands . . . the traffic was so congested that before a gal could cross the street, her dress was in danger of going out of style."

Meanwhile, the Reds were celebrating in their locker room. Tigers manager Del Baker paid a visit to congratulate Reds manager Bill McKechnie.

"The best club won, I guess," Baker told him. "If we had to lose, I'm glad we lost to you, Bill; you're a great guy." And McKechnie replied that the 1940 World Series was "the best I ever saw in all my experience in baseball."

It was a glorious moment in Cincinnati. But once again, the Reds and their fans would have to wait two more decades to experience another World Series.

## Incredible Run

*Frank McCormick performed well at the plate throughout his career but was on fire from 1938 to 1940. The Reds first baseman led the NL in hits all three seasons. He topped all NL batters with 128 RBIs in 1939 and 44 doubles in 1940. McCormick faded after that year. He batted over .300 twice as a starting player and exceeded 100 RBIs just once more before retiring in 1948.*

Catcher Ernie Lombardi was an All-Star for five consecutive years from 1936 to 1940. He was the NL MVP in 1938.

# CHAPTER 4

# STRUGGLES, STARS, AND THE SIXTIES

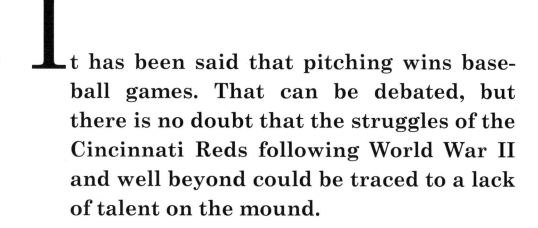

It has been said that pitching wins baseball games. That can be debated, but there is no doubt that the struggles of the Cincinnati Reds following World War II and well beyond could be traced to a lack of talent on the mound.

The team enjoyed an occasional great season from a pitcher. One example was sidearming right-hander Ewell "The Whip" Blackwell. He set an NL record for right-handers by winning 16 consecutive starts while compiling a 22–8 record in 1947. But the Reds of the late 1940s and 1950s simply could not prevent opponents from scoring. From 1945 to 1953, the Reds won more than 70 games just once and finished at least eight games under .500 every season.

The Reds did have some good hitting during that time,

Reds first baseman Ted Kluszewski hit 40 or more home runs in three consecutive years starting in 1953.

Reds pitcher Ewell Blackwell was an All-Star for six years in a row from 1946 to 1951. He led the NL with 22 wins in 1947.

though. The key batter for the Reds was burly first baseman Ted "Big Klu" Kluszewski. He hit 40 or more home runs in three consecutive years starting in 1953. He led the NL with 49 in 1954. Kluszewski was more than just a power hitter, however. He batted .300 or better in seven of eight seasons from 1949 to 1956.

Kluszewski got plenty of help from outfielder Gus Bell. He had more than 100 RBIs and scored more than 100 runs in 1953 and 1954. But the greatest boost to the offense occurred in 1956. That is when the team, temporarily known as the Redlegs, promoted a 20-year-old outfielder named Frank Robinson from the minor leagues. Robinson won Rookie of the Year honors that year. He led the NL with 122 runs while hitting 38 home runs. He remained one of the game's premier sluggers throughout his career.

The 1956 Redlegs enjoyed their first winning season since 1944. They remained in the pennant race until the final days. The team then took a step back

for several years. But in 1961, the team—again known as the Reds—won 93 games and its first pennant in 21 years. Robinson won his first of two MVP Awards. He hit .323 with 37 home runs and 123 RBIs. Meanwhile, young outfielder Vada Pinson led the league with 208 hits while batting .343.

Strong pitching helped the Reds reemerge as a title contender. The one-two punch of Jim O'Toole and Joey Jay combined for 40 wins. The bullpen duo of Bill Henry and Jim Brosnan teamed up for 32 saves.

The Reds, however, had one huge obstacle remaining. The New York Yankees awaited them in the World Series. The Reds simply were no match for the Yankees. The teams split the first two games. Then the Yankees won the last three. They outscored the Reds a combined 20–5 in the final

Hall of Famer Frank Robinson had his No. 20 retired by both the Reds and the Baltimore Orioles.

## A Tight Race

*The Reds were involved in arguably the most exciting race in baseball history in 1964. They fought in a four-team scramble that also included the St. Louis Cardinals, the Philadelphia Phillies, and the San Francisco Giants down to the final days of the season. The Reds led the NL with five games remaining, but lost four of their last five games and finished one game behind the Cardinals.*

two games at Crosley Field in Cincinnati.

In the end, the Reds understood that they were beaten by a better team. "The Yankees won the Series with a professional competence that was admirable to watch . . . if you weren't on the field losing," Brosnan wrote. ". . . Inevitably, the better club won."

The Reds remained competitive through the 1960s. They finished within four games of first place in 1962, 1964, and 1969. The team also added two of baseball's all-time greats to its lineup during that time.

One was Pete Rose. He thrived in both the infield and outfield and is generally considered the finest singles hitter in baseball history. The other was Johnny Bench. He is often regarded as the best catcher to ever play the game. The 1960s Reds also had first baseman/third baseman Tony Perez. He continued to rack up 100-RBI seasons well into the next decade.

The Reds featured several talented pitchers as well. One of them was Jim Maloney. He won at least 15 games every year from 1963 to 1968. In 1970, Gary Nolan and 20-game

## FRANK ROBINSON

Outfielder Frank Robinson remained one of the top sluggers in baseball after his Rookie of the Year season in 1956. He batted .303 with an average of 32 home runs, 101 RBIs, 104 runs, and 16 stolen bases with the Reds through 1965. But after that season, he was traded to the Baltimore Orioles for three players. None ever matched Robinson's skill level.

The Reds were criticized for the trade. Owner Bill DeWitt stated that Robinson was an "old 30" in claiming that the outfielder didn't have many good years left. But Robinson had many good years left. In fact, he won the MVP Award and earned the rare Triple Crown by leading the AL in batting average, home runs, and RBIs in his first season with the Orioles. He continued to excel well into the 1970s. He was later elected to the Baseball Hall of Fame.

## Johnny Bench

*Reds catcher Johnny Bench was a dangerous power hitter with a rocket arm behind the plate for throwing out potential base stealers. He won the NL Rookie of the Year Award in 1968. When he retired in 1983, many regarded him as the best catcher ever. Bench enjoyed six 100-plus RBI seasons, leading the league in that department three times. He hit 40 or more home runs in 1970 and 1972 and was named the NL MVP in both seasons.*

winner Jim Merritt took over as the staff aces.

That year, the Reds also emerged as the top team in the NL. They won the pennant with a 102–60 record. However, they lost to the Baltimore Orioles in the World Series. Behind Rose, Bench, Perez, and others, the Big Red Machine remained one of the top teams in the NL. However, they fell to the Oakland Athletics in the 1972 World Series and to the New York Mets in the 1973 NL Championship Series (NLCS).

It was frustrating for the team to have so much regular-season success yet always fall short in the postseason. But within three seasons, the Reds had won two World Series titles, in 1975 and 1976. The Big Red Machine era of the Reds became known as one of the best baseball teams ever. Little did anyone imagine that the Reds would return to the Fall Classic just one more time through the 2010 season.

Manager Sparky Anderson guided the Reds to World Series titles in 1975 and 1976. The Reds compiled a 14–3 combined record in the postseason during those two years.

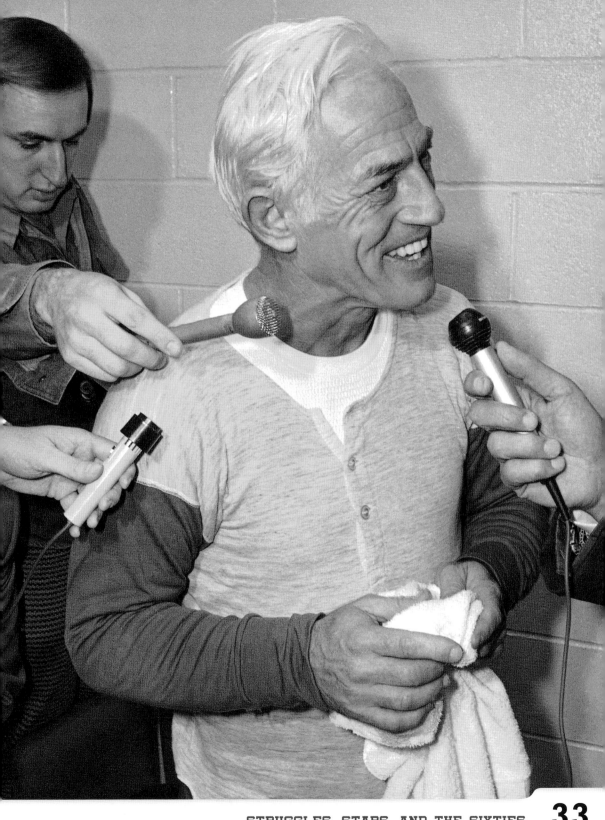

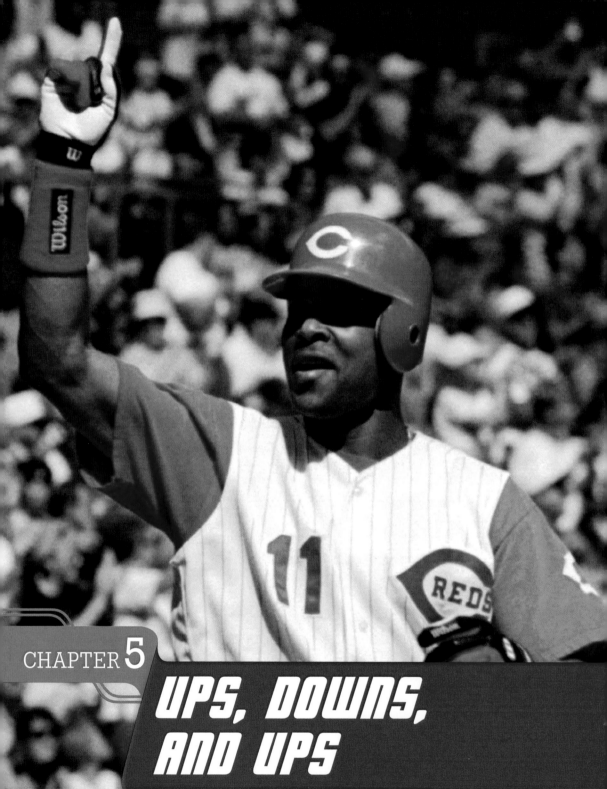

# CHAPTER 5

# UPS, DOWNS, AND UPS

**I**t was only a matter of time before the Big Red Machine broke down. By 1979, Pete Rose had signed with the Philadelphia Phillies. Tony Perez had been traded to the Montreal Expos. Meanwhile, Johnny Bench and Joe Morgan were fading toward the end of their careers.

The Reds still had enough talent to snag the 1979 division title. However, they lost three straight to eventual World Series champions the Pittsburgh Pirates in the NLCS. After that, the Big Red Machine era was officially finished.

The Reds lost a franchise-record 101 games in 1982. Rose came back to play for and manage the team midway through the 1984 season. The team rebounded under Rose and won at least 84 games each year from 1985 to 1988. Veteran slugger Dave Parker averaged 30 home runs and 113 RBIs during a three-year stretch from 1985 to 1987. But it was the addition

Cincinnati native Barry Larkin, the 1995 NL MVP, once hit a total of five home runs in two consecutive games. The shortstop played for the Reds from 1986 to 2004.

## BANNED

Pete Rose played for his hometown team from 1963 to 1978, then again as player/manager in the mid-1980s. As a player, he led the NL in hits seven times, doubles five times, and runs four times. He finished his career as baseball's all-time leader in hits with 4,256, second in doubles with 746, and sixth in runs scored with 2,165. Rose was known for hustling and trying his hardest on every play. He was a sure bet to be voted into the Baseball Hall of Fame on the first ballot.

But in early 1989, an MLB investigation concluded that Rose had bet on baseball games while managing the Reds. Rose denied it, but agreed to a lifetime ban from the sport. During a television interview in 2003, Rose admitted that he had gambled on baseball. He remains banned from the sport. He is also ineligible to be voted into the Hall of Fame.

of young players who really turned the Reds around.

Versatile outfielder Eric Davis combined blazing speed with raw power. But he peaked early. His production slipped after he stole 80 bases in 1986 and hit 37 home runs the following year. Position players such as shortstop Barry Larkin, third baseman Chris Sabo, and outfielder Paul O'Neill were not up to Big Red Machine standards, but they gave Reds fans hope.

So did a young starting pitching staff that included left-hander Tom Browning. He won 20 games in 1985. He also threw the only perfect game in Reds history in 1988.

The Reds named feisty Lou Piniella as manager in 1990. An equally feisty bullpen trio emerged around the same time. The three struck fear into opposing hitters

Tom Browning threw the only perfect game in Reds history against the Los Angeles Dodgers at Riverfront Stadium on September 16, 1988.

whenever they strolled toward the mound.

Left-handers Randy Myers and Norm Charlton and right-hander Rob Dibble were known as the "Nasty Boys." Their nickname did not come solely from the "nasty" fastballs that sped toward the plate at 95 to 100 miles per hour. The trio also gained that nickname for their willingness to fire the ball inside or to even hit batters with pitches.

"We were pretty much mean," Charlton said. "If you looked at us wrong, we would try to hit you."

Pitcher Jose Rijo waves to the crowd after the Reds swept the Oakland Athletics in the 1990 World Series.

Most of the time, they were just getting batters out. Myers led the team with 31 saves. Charlton won 12 games as a starter and reliever. Dibble struck out 136 batters in just 98 innings.

The 1990 Reds won their division and upset the Pirates to earn their first NL pennant in 14 years. Awaiting them in the World Series was the Oakland Athletics. The A's had won 103 games during the regular season. They featured sluggers Mark McGwire and Jose Canseco and had the best pitching staff in the league.

The A's reached the World Series by winning four straight from the Boston Red Sox in the AL Championship Series. Most believed the A's would crush the Reds.

Quite the opposite occurred. The Reds outscored the A's 22–8 in a four-game sweep. Sabo hit two home runs in the Series, both in Game 3. The Nasty Boys made seven appearances and gave up no runs. But the pitching hero was starter Jose Rijo. He won the first and final games of the Series. Rijo gave up just one run in 15 1/3 innings.

Nobody was happier to win than Browning. He won a World Series title and had a son named Tucker born during the Series triumph.

"I can't wait to tell Tucker that he was born while we were becoming world champions," he said with a laugh after

## Coming Home

Ken Griffey played for the Reds during the Big Red Machine era of the 1970s. His son, Ken Griffey Jr., became one of baseball's best—and most popular—players with the Seattle Mariners in the 1990s. Griffey Jr. was a certain future Hall of Famer when the Reds traded for him in 2000. Although he enjoyed a few strong years back in his hometown, he was slowed by injuries and age. He played with the Reds into the 2008 season. He was traded to the Chicago White Sox and finished his career back with the Mariners in 2010.

Game 4. "World champions. Kind of has a nice ring to it, don't you think?"

The Reds dropped off after the 1991 season. They finished 74–88 and fifth out of six teams in the NL West. After some inconsistency they returned to the playoffs in 1995. The Reds swept the Los Angeles Dodgers in the first round. However, the Atlanta Braves swept the Reds in the NLCS.

The Reds were an average team for the next five years. In 1999, they finished 96–67 and 1 1/2 games out of first place. They lost a one-game playoff for a wild-card berth to the New York Mets. But they soon fell into a decade of struggles. The Reds did not have any winning seasons from 2001 to 2009.

Things finally began to turn around for the Reds late in the decade. The team hired manager Dusty Baker in 2008.

He had guided the San Francisco Giants to seven winning seasons and to the 2002 NL pennant. Behind a mix of talented young players and established veterans, the Reds finally produced another winning season in 2010.

Young first baseman Joey Votto emerged as an elite player and a Triple Crown contender. He was named the NL MVP after batting .324 with 113 RBIs and 37 homers. He combined with second baseman Brandon Phillips and veterans like third baseman Scott Rolen and catcher Ramon Hernandez to give the Reds the top scoring offense in the NL.

A pitching staff featuring young hurlers Johnny Cueto and Mike Leake and veteran Bronson Arroyo helped the Reds stay above the favored St. Louis Cardinals in the NL Central Division. Their 91–71

Second baseman Brandon Phillips, *right*, and third baseman Scott Rolen produced All-Star seasons to help the Reds return to the playoffs in 2010.

record was their best since 1999.

The Reds returned to the postseason for the first time since 1995. But their breakout season ended there. The two-time defending NL champions the Philadelphia Phillies swept the Reds in three games. But with a strong core of young players like Votto, Cueto, and Leake leading the way, the Reds have given fans reason for optimism once again.

# TIMELINE

|  |  |
|------|-------|
| 1869 | The Red Stockings complete their first season as the first professional baseball team in the United States undefeated with a 17–8 defeat of the Mutuals of New York on November 6. |
| 1876 | The new NL accepts the Red Stockings as a charter member. |
| 1882 | A new Red Stockings team begins playing in the upstart American Association. They join the NL in 1890. |
| 1919 | The Reds complete an eight-game World Series win over the Chicago White Sox, but the triumph is tainted when it is learned a year later that several members of the Sox had taken bribes to lose on purpose. |
| 1935 | On May 24, the Reds host the first night game in MLB history, defeating the Philadelphia Phillies at Crosley Field before more than 20,000 fans. |
| 1938 | The Reds' Johnny Vander Meer becomes the only pitcher to throw back-to-back no-hitters, blanking the Boston Bees on June 11 and the Brooklyn Dodgers on June 15. |
| 1939 | The Reds clinch their first NL pennant in 20 years with a 5–3 win over the St. Louis Cardinals on September 28. |
| 1940 | The Reds win their first untainted World Series triumph on October 8 with a 2–1 defeat of the Detroit Tigers. |
| 1956 | Behind Frank Robinson and Ted "Big Klu" Kluszewski, the Reds set a team record by slugging 221 home runs. |

| | |
|---|---|
| **1961** | The Reds clinch the pennant on September 26, but lose a five-game World Series to the New York Yankees. |
| **1965** | Slugger Frank Robinson is traded to the Baltimore Orioles on December 9 for pitcher Milt Pappas and two others. |
| **1970** | The Reds unveil new Riverfront Stadium on June 30 with an 8–2 loss to the Atlanta Braves. They reach the World Series but lose to the Orioles. |
| **1972** | The Reds beat the Pittsburgh Pirates in the NLCS, but drop the World Series to the Oakland Athletics. |
| **1975** | In Game 7 on October 22, the Reds earn their first World Series triumph in 35 years with a 4–3 defeat of the Boston Red Sox. |
| **1976** | The Reds win two straight World Series for the first time in franchise history by defeating the Yankees on October 21. |
| **1990** | The Reds stun baseball with a four-game sweep of heavily favored Athletics in the World Series, completing the triumph on October 20. |
| **2003** | The Great American Ball Park opens on March 31 with a 10–1 Reds loss to the Pirates. |
| **2010** | After nine losing seasons, young first baseman Joey Votto leads the Reds to a 91–71 record and the NL Central title. However, the Phillies sweep the Reds in the NL Division Series. |

# QUICK STATS

## FRANCHISE HISTORY
Cincinnati Red Stockings (1882–89)
Cincinnati Redlegs (1954–59)
Cincinnati Reds (1890–1953, 1960– )

## WORLD SERIES
*(wins in bold)*
**1919**, 1939, **1940**, 1961, 1970, 1972,
**1975**, **1976**, **1990**

## NL CHAMPIONSHIP SERIES
*(1969– )*
1970, 1972, 1973, 1975, 1976, 1979,
1990, 1995

## DIVISION CHAMPIONSHIPS
*(1969– )*
1970, 1972, 1973, 1975, 1976, 1979,
1990, 1995, 2010

## KEY PLAYERS
*(position[s]; seasons with team)*
Johnny Bench (C; 1967–83)
George Foster (OF; 1971–81)
Barry Larkin (SS; 1986–2004)
Ernie Lombardi (C; 1932–41)
Joe Morgan (2B; 1972–79)
Tony Perez (3B/1B; 1964–76,
    1984–86)
Eppa Rixey (SP; 1921–33)
Frank Robinson (OF; 1956–65)
Pete Rose (2B/3B/OF; 1963–78,
    1984–86)
Edd Roush (OF; 1916–26, 1931)
Joey Votto (1B; 2007– )

## KEY MANAGERS
Sparky Anderson (1970–78):
    863–586; 26–16 (postseason)
Bill McKechnie (1938–46):
    744–631; 4–7 (postseason)

## HOME PARKS
Bank Street Grounds (1882–83)
League Park I (1884–93)
League Park II (1894–1901)
Palace of the Fans (1902–11)
Redland Field/Crosley Field (1912–70)
Riverfront Stadium/Cinergy Field
    (1970–2002)
Great American Ball Park (2003– )

* All statistics through 2010 season

# QUOTES AND ANECDOTES

The fledgling American Association was founded in Cincinnati in 1881. The meeting that made it official was held at the Gibson Hotel in that city.

It was fortunate that the baseball season was more than two months away on January 27, 1937. That's when the flooding of a local creek caused the playing surface at Crosley Field to be submerged under 21 feet (6.40 m) of water. Reds pitcher Lee Grissom and groundskeeper Matty Schwab were photographed in a rowboat crossing the playing surface.

In what can best be described as a marathon, the 1967 Reds participated in the longest game in franchise history on September 1. It took 21 innings for them to lose to the San Francisco Giants, 1–0.

Did Pete Rose work hard on the baseball diamond? All-time great slugger Hank Aaron once offered his opinion. "Does [Rose] hustle?" he asked. "Before the All-Star game he came into the clubhouse and took off his shoes and they ran another mile without him."

Jim Brosnan was a decent relief pitcher for the Reds in the early 1960s. But he gained far more fame as a book writer. His 1959 diary titled *The Long Season* was controversial for its time because it described events on and off the field that some felt shouldn't have been revealed. It also surprised many that a player could write his own book and do it so well. "I had actually written the book by myself, thus trampling upon the tradition that a player should hire a sportswriter to do the work," Brosnan said. "I was, on these accounts, a sneak and a snob."

# GLOSSARY

**ace**

A team's best starting pitcher.

**attendance**

The number of fans who come to watch a team play during a particular season or game.

**clinch**

To officially settle something, such as a berth in the playoffs.

**contender**

A team that is in the race for a championship or playoff berth.

**franchise**

An entire sports organization, including the players, coaches, and staff.

**general manager**

The executive who is in charge of the team's overall operation. He or she hires and fires managers and coaches, drafts players, and signs free agents.

**pennant**

A flag. In baseball, it symbolizes that a team has won its league championship.

**postseason**

The games in which the best teams play after the regular-season schedule has been completed.

**retire**

To officially end one's career.

**rookie**

A first-year player in the major leagues.

**tradition**

Something that is handed down.

**wild card**

Playoff berths given to the best remaining teams that did not win their respective divisions.

# FOR MORE INFORMATION

## Further Reading

Bench, Johnny. *From Behind the Plate*. New York: Prentice-Hall, 1972.

Brosnan, Jim. *The Long Season*. Lanham, MD: Ivan R. Dee, 2002.

Shannon, Mike. *The Good, the Bad and the Ugly Cincinnati Reds*. Chicago: Triumph Books, 2008.

Stallard, Mark (editor). *Echoes of Cincinnati Reds Baseball: The Greatest Stories Ever Told*. Chicago: Triumph Books, 2007.

## Web Links

To learn more about the Cincinnati Reds, visit ABDO Publishing Company online at **www.abdopublishing.com**. Web sites about the Reds are featured on our Book Links page. These links are routinely monitored and updated to provide the most current information available.

## Places To Visit

**Cincinnati Reds Hall of Fame and Museum**
100 Main Street
Cincinnati, OH 45202
513-765-7576
mlb.mlb.com/cin/hof/index.jsp
The Reds Hall of Fame and Museum honors the greatest players and teams in franchise history with a number of artifacts and exhibits.

**The Great American Ball Park**
100 Joe Nuxhall Way
Cincinnati, OH 45202
513-381-REDS (7337)
This has been the Reds' home field since 2003. Tours are available when the Reds are not playing.

**National Baseball Hall of Fame and Museum**
25 Main Street
Cooperstown, NY 13326
1-888-HALL-OF-FAME
www.baseballhall.org
This hall of fame and museum highlights the greatest players and moments in the history of baseball. Johnny Bench, Joe Morgan, and Frank Robinson are among the former Reds enshrined here.

# INDEX

## About The Author

Marty Gitlin is a freelance writer based in Cleveland, Ohio. He has written more than 25 educational books. Gitlin has won more than 45 awards during his 25 years as a writer, including first place for general excellence from the Associated Press. He lives with his wife and three children in Ohio.